Places We Live

Living in a
City

Ellen Labrecque

raintree
a Capstone company — publishers for children

Raintree is an imprint of Capstone Global Library Limited, a company incorporated in England and Wales having its registered office at 7 Pilgrim Street, London, EC4V 6LB –
Registered company number: 6695582

www.raintree.co.uk
myorders@raintree.co.uk

Edited by James Benefield and Brenda Haugen
Designed by Richard Parker
Illustrations by HL Studios
Original illustrations © Capstone Global Library Ltd 2015
Picture research by Jo Miller
Production by Helen McCreath
Originated by Capstone Global Library Ltd
Printed and bound in China

ISBN 978 1 406 28778 3
18 17 16 15 14
10 9 8 7 6 5 4 3 2 1

British Library Cataloguing in Publication Data
A full catalogue record for this book is available from the British Library.

Acknowledgements
We would like to thank the following for reproducing photographs: Alamy: Guy Croft, 20, Marcelo Rudini, 21, Travel Pictures, 17; Getty Images: Photolibrary/Robin Smith, 15; Newscom: akg-images, 8, Danita Delimont Photography/Jaynes Gallery/Bill Young, 10, Getty Images/ AFP/Peter Parks, 25; Shutterstock: Ana Phelps, 23, Shutterstock/claudio zaccherini, 26, Shutterstock/Eric Broder Van Dyke, 13, Shutterstock/ EUROPHOTOS, 4, Shutterstock/gary yim, 11, Shutterstock/Lewis Tse Pui Lung, 24, Shutterstock/Lukiyanova Natalia / frenta, 19, Shutterstock/Mazzzur, 12, Shutterstock/nodff, 18, Shutterstock/Pete Spiro, 27, Shutterstock/ptnphoto, 5, Shutterstock/serato, 16, Shutterstock/testing, cover, Shutterstock/Vacclav, 9; SuperStock: age fotostock/Tibor Bognár, 7; UIG via Getty Images: Education Images, 22.

Design Elements: Shutterstock: donatas1205, Olympus.

We would like to thank Rachel Bowles for her invaluable help in the preparation of this book.

Every effort has been made to contact copyright holders of material reproduced in this book. Any omissions will be rectified in subsequent printings if notice is given to the publisher.

Contents

Some words are shown in bold, **like this**. You can find out what they mean by looking in the glossary.

What is a city?

A city is an **urban settlement**. Lots of people work and live close together here. There are lots of important things here, too. This could include **places of worship**, universities, shops, museums, and company and **government** offices.

Over 13 million people live in the centre of Tokyo, Japan.

Even small cities are places full of life and action.

Cities mean different things to people around the world. People who live in **rural** areas could call a place with 5,000 people a city. In some areas of the world, 5,000 people might fill just one school or office building.

Where are cities?

Cities start in places which meet people's basic needs. For example, every city needs water for its people. This means many cities are built near rivers. Rivers provide water and also transport for the people who live there.

Cities with the most people

		Population
1.	Tokyo, Japan	13,300,000
2.	Seoul, South Korea	10,000,000
3.	Jakarta, Indonesia	9,500,000

The city of Seoul, Korea, is built beside the Han River.

City people need food to eat, too. A city built near water means nearby land is usually **fertile**. Gardens and farms can grow vegetables for city people. If city people need anything else, boats and ships can transport this to them.

Cities of the past

In early times, many cities were built on hills or near water. If enemies tried to attack, they could easily be seen from the hills or in the water. Rome and Jerusalem are cities that were first built long ago. They were both built on hills.

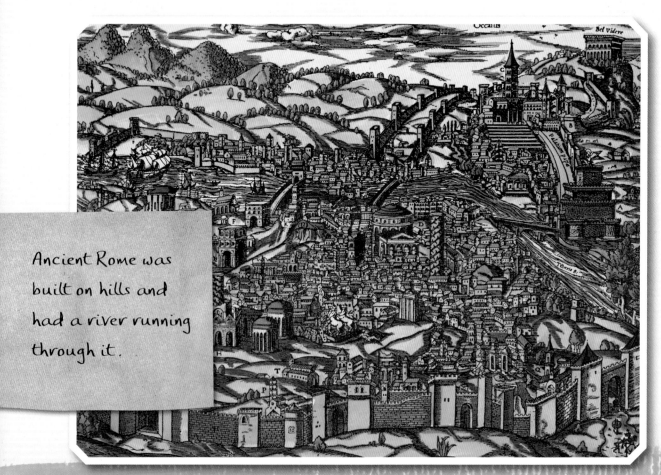

Ancient Rome was built on hills and had a river running through it.

George Washington helped to pick where the White House was built, but he never actually lived there.

Some cities were built by the people in power at the time. The first president of the USA, George Washington, helped to pick Washington DC as the capital city. It was near to where he already lived.

Why do people live in cities today?

People often move to cities because they could offer people better lives. For example, a city has a better variety of jobs than in a **rural** area. Many cities also have excellent schools and universities.

People move to Dubai, United Arab Emirates, for jobs in banking and construction.

You don't need to worry about traffic if you're taking this monorail in Sydney, Australia.

There are lots of ways to get around in cities. You can get public transport to places inside the city or outside of it. There can be many roads for people with cars, too. But if a city is too crowded, there can be traffic problems.

All kinds of people

Over half of the people in the world live in cities. They are filled with both rich and poor people. Some of the richest people in the world live right next to some of the poorest people.

In Mumbai, India, half of the city's people are poor.

There are homeless people all over the world.

Some rich city people live in large, expensively built homes. Very poor people live in tiny **slums** they have built themselves using scrap material. The poorest could be homeless and live on the streets.

City puzzle

Cities are made up of different parts. They fit together like giant jigsaw puzzles. The centre of a city usually has offices for businesses and **government**. There are also large areas for shopping and entertainment.

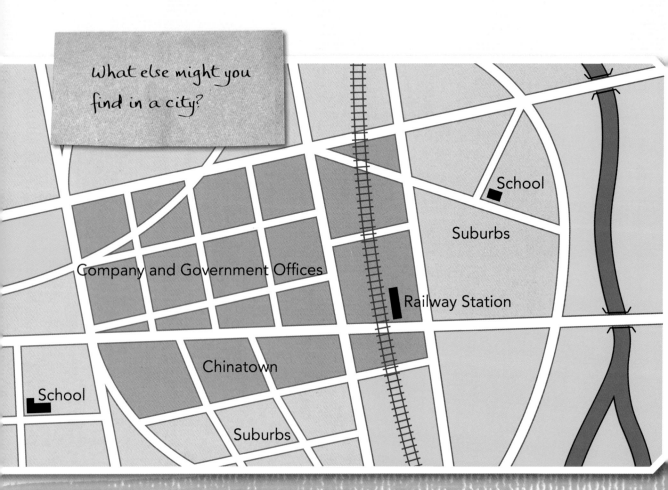

What else might you find in a city?

School

Suburbs

Company and Government Offices

Railway Station

Chinatown

School

Suburbs

Not everyone lives in the suburbs. Some people live right in the city, such as in a Chinatown.

Towns or areas that are located outside a city are called **suburbs**. This is where a lot of people's homes are. Many people live in the suburbs and come into the centre of a city to work. These people are called **commuters**.

Under our feet

In big cities there are things happening underground, too. For example, when people flush a toilet the water and waste ends up in small underground tunnels called **sewers**.

City planners are always careful to keep drinking water pipes separate from waste pipes.

The underground Moscow Metro System in Russia is one of the busiest in the world.

Some big cities have underground transport systems to get people around. This cuts down on traffic on the crowded city streets. It can be the quickest way to get about, too. You don't get traffic jams underground.

Buildings and landmarks

Sometimes city buildings are bult tall because there is not much space. Office and living space is added by building up, not out! The tallest building in the world is the Burj Khalifa in the city of Dubai, United Arab Emirates.

The Burj Khalifa rises 828 metres (2,217 feet) in the air.

Tourists like to visit cities to see famous **landmarks**. Tourists stay in the city's hotels and eat in the restaurants. They buy gifts to remember their visits. This all helps to make cities richer.

Open spaces

Even though cities are crowded, people have built or kept space for parks, gardens and even beaches. Central Park in New York City, USA, is one of the most famous **green spaces** found in a city in the whole world.

Central Park is filled with pathways, playground and lakes.

Curitiba, Brazil, has increased green space from 1 square metre per person to 52 square metres per person in 30 years!

City planners are now trying to create more and more green spaces than before. Parks and lakes make people relaxed and give them places to exercise to stay healthy, too.

Fun things to do

Cities are packed with fun things to do. For example, they are home to some great zoos. The Moscow Zoo in Moscow, Russia, has over 6,000 animals. Cities also have many great museums and indoor places to play.

San Diego Zoo, USA, is one of the most famous zoos in the world.

The 2016 Olympics in Rio de Janeiro, Brazil, has brought lots of attention to the city.

Cities host all kinds of events, from concerts to sporting competitions. When a city hosts a special event, lots of new buildings are built, such as stadiums.

City life

Living in a city can be exciting, but hard, too. Sometimes it is difficult to find a home that is **affordable** and big enough for the entire family. Many cities are crowded. This can make it hard to walk or drive from one place to another.

Cities are filled with many people fighting for the same space.

Some people in the city of Beijing, China, wear masks. They think this will protect them from the smog.

Cities can also harm people's health. Sometimes the air in cities becomes polluted by traffic and factories. **Smog** can hang over cities and make it hard to breathe and make people ill.

Cities of the future

Cities are now very crowded. In 1900, only 16 cities had more than 1 million people living in them. Today, there are more than 400 cities with this many people. What will happen when there are too many people?

Shanghai, China, is the fastest growing city in the world.

Some cities, such as London, try to get people to ride bikes instead of drive cars.

City planners work to improve cities and make them "greener" places to live. This means they try to cut down on the city's waste. They build new buildings that use **solar power** instead of power from gas, oil or coal.

Fun facts

- London (England), Paris (France), New York City (USA) and Bangkok (Thailand) are the most visited cities in the world.

- Washington DC, USA, is a city that was built on swamp land.

- The London underground system is called the Tube. It was the world's first underground railway.

- A megacity is a city with more than 10 million people living in it. Tokyo in Japan and Seoul in South Korea are both megacities.

- Singapore in Southeast Asia is a city and a country! It is called a city-state.

- Vatican City is also a city-state. It is also the smallest country in the world. It is located inside the city of Rome, Italy.

Quiz

Are each of these sentences true or false?

1. People live in cities because they like to enjoy the wide-open spaces.
2. Towns and areas right outside a city are called suburbs.
3. Central Park in New York City is packed with buildings.
4. There is nothing fun to do in cities.
5. In the past, cities were built on hills.

5. True. This made it easier to protect if the city came under attack.

4. False. The city is filled with fun things for kids to do.

3. False. Central Park is a wide-open green space.

2. True.

1. False. People live in cities because it is easy to find and do all the things they want.

Glossary

affordable something people have enough money to buy

commuter person who travels some way between home and work

fertile land that can grow food, usually with deep and good soil

government group of people who run a city, town or country

green space parks and other open areas with lots of grass, plants and trees

landmark famous building, structure or green space

place of worship religious building for people to pray and meet in

rural area outside a city or town, usually farmland with few people and buildings

settlement place where people live permanently, such as a village, town or city

sewer underground passageway carrying people's poo and wee

slum overcrowded area where poor people live, often without running water and electricity

smog fog combined with air pollution, which is harmful to health

solar power energy that uses the sun's rays to make electricity

suburb town or area right outside of a city, where people live

tourist person who visits another place for fun

urban to do with living in a town or city

Find out more

Books

A City Through Time, Steve Noon (Dorling Kindersley, 2013)

City, Philip Steele (Dorling Kindersley, 2011)

City Across Time, Peter Kent (Kingfisher Books, 2010)

Living in a City (Our Local Area), Richard Spilsbury
    (Raintree, 2010)

Websites

You can find more city facts and learn more about interesting places to live around the world by exploring these websites:

www.bbc.co.uk/schools/primaryhistory/romans/city_of_rome/
Learn more about the ancient city of Rome here.

http://kids.tate.org.uk/games/my-imaginary-city
Visit this website and invent your own city!

http://projectbritain.com/regions/london.htm
Find out more facts and figures about the UK's capital city, London, on this website.

www.worldatlas.com/citypops.htm
This site is great for checking out city populations.

Index